BIKING IN VIKINGLAND

Where to Go
What to Expect
How to Get There

by
MARLYS MICKELSON

ISBN 0-9620610-2-6

Also by Marlys Mickelson
SEAT YOURSELF
A Complete Guide to Twin Cities Arenas,
Auditoriums and Theatres
First printing in 1988. Second printing 1990.

Front cover photo: Paul Sundberg, Two Harbors, MN
Back cover photo: DNR photo, Dan Ruda

This book is dedicated to a diverse group of energetic individuals whose mutual interest in physical activity, ecology, conservation and the great outdoors evolved into an ever-widening circle of friends who call themselves the *Weakenders.* ™

ACKNOWLEDGEMENTS

My sincere appreciation for the cooperation and assistance given by the Minnesota Department of Transportation, Department of Natural Resources and Department of Tourism.

And especially to my husband Phil for his support and assistance.

INTRODUCTION

If you like bicycling and everything that goes with it -- good exercise, friendship and being outdoors -- you'll love this book.

This easy-to-use guide highlights improved, off-highway routes specifically designated for biking and hiking.

Whatever your age or biking skill, this guide is for individuals, groups or families who want to bike at their leisure on trails that don't mean spending an entire day on a bicycle seat.

In the trail section, we've put together comprehensive trail maps, trail length and other pertinent trailhead information. Attractions in surrounding communities are listed, too.

Biking in Vikingland tells you where to go, what to expect and how to get there.

In Celebration of Cycling

TO WHEEL quietly up and down hill and across the valley, miles away from so-called civilization, and yet knowing that with a good bicycle miles mean but little; to wheel along drinking in the perfumes of the morning with the song of the birds, and at even, thankful for the matchless glow in the west and the music of cow-bells; to wheel silently at sunset into some peaceful village where your guidebook bids you expect a welcome — all this is worth celebrating.

— Philip C. Hubert, Jr.,
Scribner's Magazine, *1895*

CONTENTS

PART I

AN OVERVIEW

Minnesota Department
of Transportation
Bikeways

Addresses
Phone Numbers
Accommodations

Wisconsin Addresses
Phone Numbers

Biking in Vikingland can happen in many different ways, in many different places, requiring all degrees of skill and endurance. Although the emphasis of this book is primarily off-road bike trails, the biking enthusiast should be aware of the many alternatives offered by Minnesota and Wisconsin.

For the most comprehensive and detailed information and maps on biking in Minnesota and Wisconsin, we can refer you to no better source than the *Explore Minnesota Bikeways* maps published by the Minnesota Department of Transportation and the *Bicycle Escape Guide* published by the Wisconsin Division of Tourism.

Minnesota Bikeways maps divide the state into four sec-tions and the metro area into two sections. At the present time only four of the six are available. You may order the northeast, southeast, metro east and metro west by mail. The northwest section is in the planning stage and will be available in 1991. **For state areas not covered by the maps now available (example southwest area) telephone Department of Transportation maps section at 612-296-2216.**

In addition to the DNR-maintained trails which are detailed in Part II of this book, you will find accurate maps of trails and paths in county and state parks, cities and routes on the state highways which are suited for biking and of particular interest to long distance riders. Trails and roads are color coded to iden-tify suitability for your plans. Your investment in each of these maps would be well worth the cost. In addition to mail order, the Department of Transportation maps are avail-able in bike stores and some map stores.

In addition to the metro east and metro west maps, the four state section maps include cities with designated bikeways. Some of these are off-street paths. Off-street bike paths in northeast Minnesota are located in these cities: Duluth, Grand Rapids, Hibbing and Virginia. In the southeast, cities with off-street biking are Faribault, Mankato, Owatonna, Red Wing, Rochester, St. Cloud and Winona. Cities in the western half of the state with off-street bike paths include: Detroit Lakes, Fairmont, Fergus Falls, Marshall, Moorhead, Park Rapids and Walker.

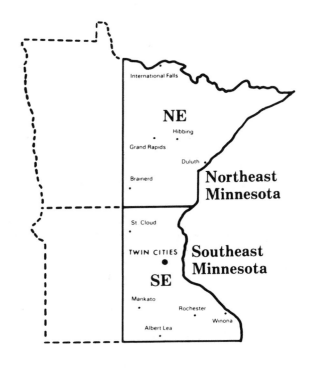

Each map contains information regarding:

- Road analysis for bicycle usage
- Location of paved road shoulders
- Location of off-road bikeways
- Location of bike-pedestrian bridges
- Controlled access roads (bicycles prohibited)
- Unpaved/gravel roads
- Historical and cultural attractions
- Public parklands and facilities

Map Price Schedule
(includes tax)

MAP	QUANTITY	
	1-19	20 or more
Southeast (SE)	$3.00 ea.	$2.40 ea.
Northeast (NE)	$3.00 ea.	$2.40 ea.
Metro East	$2.00 ea.	$1.60 ea.
Metro West	$2.00 ea.	$1.60 ea.
Postage per *order*	$1.00	$2.00

Prices subject to change without notice.

Mail Map Orders To:

Minnesota Department of Transportation
John Ireland Boulevard
Room B-20
St. Paul MN 55155
612-296-2216

or

Minnesota State Documents Center
117 University Avenue (Ford Bldg.)
St. Paul MN 55155
612-297-3000

Minnesota is biking country. It is the leader in the development of bicycle trails with 570 miles of bike paths available to approximately 2.8 million riders. Minnesota is one of 24 states with a full-time bike coordinator. For additional information, safety brochures, etc., contact:

State Bicycle Coordinator
State Bicycle Advisory Board
807 Transportation Building
St. Paul MN 55155
612-297-1838

The Minnesota Department of Natural Resources has converted 250 miles of railroad right-of-way that offer a quiet biking experience through scenic areas on a level, less than three percent grade. Parking space is provided and rest areas generally include a picnic area, drinking water and toilets. Individual maps of the eight bicycle trails and state parks with bicycle paths are available at no charge. Contact:

Minnesota Department of Natural Resources
Outdoor Information Center
Box 40, 500 Lafayette Road
St. Paul MN 55146
612-296-6699
Within Minnesota, Toll Free: 800-652-9747

The Department of Natural Resources Trails and Waterways Division distributes its publication *Minnesota Trail Explorer* eight times annually. Two issues are dedicated solely to biking and feature self-guided tour routes. Contact:

Trail Explorer
DNR - Trails and Waterways Unit
Box 52 - 500 Lafayette Road
St. Paul MN   55155-4052

MINNESOTA INFORMATION

The DNR State Trails featured in Part II are suitable for wheelchairs and families with young children. Many trails are ideal for family nature studies. Shop carefully for the child carrier that you attach to your bicycle and be certain the youngster is wearing a helmet. Remember to stock water and energy boosters, and that small wheels require many more revolutions than your 27" bicycle.

The Minnesota Department of Tourism has developed two free directories for accommodations that you may order by mail or phone. *Explore Minnesota Hotels/Motels* and *Explore Minnesota Bed and Breakfast and Historic Inns* are available from:

> Minnesota Office of Tourism
> 250 Skyway Level
> 375 Jackson Street
> St. Paul MN 55101
> 800-657-3700
> Metro area: 296-5029

Another guide to bed and breakfast accommodations is available at your bookstore or directly from the publisher:

> *Room at the Inn Minnesota:*
> *Guide to Minnesota's Historic B & B's,*
> *Hotels and Country Inns*
> by Laura Zahn
> Down to Earth Publications
> 1426 Sheldon
> St. Paul MN 55108
> 800-888-9653

Wisconsin maintains eight trails for bicycling, a total of nearly 200 miles. Most of these bike trails are surfaced with crushed limestone. Wisconsin has a daily fee of $1.50 resident and $2.00 non-resident. The trails are open from 6:00 a.m. to 11 p.m. For a copy of *Biking Wisconsin's State Park Trails*, send $3.00 to:

> Wisconsin DNR Bureau of
> Parks and Recreation
> P.O. Box 7921
> Madison WI 53707-7921
> 608-266-2181

The Wisconsin State Parks brochure *Explore and Enjoy* is available at that address, too.

The State of Wisconsin publishes two maps exclusively devoted to biking, one for each half of the state. Either or both are available at no charge. For the *Western Wisconsin Bicycle Escape Guide* and/or *Eastern Wisconsin Bicycle Escape Guide* contact:

> Wisconsin Division of Tourism
> 123 West Washington Avenue
> P.O. Box 7606
> Madison WI 53707
> 800-372-2737

We have included two of our favorite Wisconsin trails in Part IV.

PART II

STATE TRAILS

Cannon Valley Trail

Douglas State Trail

Heartland State Trail

Hinckley Fire State Trail

Luce Line State Trail

Willard Munger State Trail

Root River State Trail

Sakatah Singing Hills State Trail

Trail length: 19.7 miles

Surface: 12 miles blacktop,
7.7 miles crushed limestone

Trailhead east: Old W. Main St. and Bench St. one block off Hwy. 61 in west Red Wing. Parking lot nearby. To downtown Red Wing, you may follow Old West Main along the marked historic route near the Mississippi River.

In the area: Visit the beautifully restored St. James Hotel. Consider a Mississippi River cruise on the Princess Red Wing (May - October). For more information on attractions in the area, write to:

Red Wing Area Chamber of Commerce
416 Bush St.
Red Wing MN 55066
612-238-4719

Trailhead west: Although the trail actually starts near 3rd Street in Cannon Falls, parking is limited. Ample parking is available across from the ballpark on E. Stoughton St. Trail access is provided from the east end of the lot.

In the area: Canoeing and tubing on the Cannon River. For more information, write or call:

Cannon Falls Area Chamber of Commerce
103 - 4th St. North
Cannon Falls MN 55009
507-263-2289

For a trail with great scenery in all seasons, shelter from the wind and shade from the hot sun, this is the place to be. The trail follows the Cannon River Valley from Cannon Falls to Red Wing. At 19.7 miles, it is a short one-way ride or a quite manageable two-way trip. Although not a part of the DNR State Trail system, this is a scenic, well-maintained trail, most of which is now paved. Only two stretches, totaling about 8 miles, are crushed limestone and it is the intention of the Joint Powers Board of Cannon Falls, Red Wing and Goodhue County, to complete this paving as rapidly as funding permits.

For this gem, we are indebted to a group of private citizens from Cannon Falls, Welch and Red Wing who saw the recreational value of the area. They secured the property and obtained the grants and assistance to improve it and replace the numerous bridges you will cross. The trail parallels the river along the south side between bluffs and trees with few stretches of open country. The many bridges tell the rider there are a lot of gorges and feeder streams which empty into the Cannon River.

If you plan to ride both ways on your day, we recommend starting at Red Wing where there is a parking lot near the beginning of the trail just off old West Main St. This gives you an opportunity to explore Red Wing with its old river-town flavor. It also gives you the benefit of the slight downhill grade on the last half of the trip, rather than the first half. Along the way, you will find picnic tables about 3½ miles east of Cannon Falls, and portable restrooms at approximately 1/3 distance intervals. Refreshments in the village of Welch are available if you wish to take a short side trip.

Riders will see an occasional metal pipe rigged for donations. We suggest you take a bill or two with you. Your contribution will help the association with maintenance and improvements. In 1990 they plan to pave an extension from the trail in west Red Wing over to A.P. Anderson Park which will make park facilities available to bikers.

Whether this is your first visit or a repeat ride, you will likely want to do this one many times.

Administered by a Joint Powers Board from
Cannon Falls, Red Wing and Goodhue County.

61

A N

LCH

R

Cannon River

90

93

Spring Creek

RED WING

85

Bench St.

1

19

➤ Mileage
π Picnic
P Parking
W Water
R Restrooms

7

VASA

91

Mississippi River

61

63

92

Tyler Rd.

Bench St. access
93

(trail
extension
to Lower A.P.
π Anderson Park)
P W R

P

Bay Pt. Park

W R P

Old W. Main St.

RED WING

Bench St.

1

Trail length: 12.5 miles

Surface: Blacktop

Access includes three separate parking lots
with rest facilities.

Trailhead south: About 2 miles NW of Rochester on Co. Rd. 4,
or if you are driving on Hwy. 52 take the IBM exit west to Co.
Rd. 4. There is ample paved parking, shelter and portable
restrooms.

In the area: Rochester has many areas of interest including
the Mayo Clinic and Museum, Mayowood and the 30,000 giant
Canada geese that live at Silver Lake Park. Bring a bag of
bread and wear shoes. You can write or call for more
information:

> Rochester Visitors Bureau
> 220 South Broadway, Suite 100
> Rochester MN 55902
> 800-426-6025

Mid access: Douglas on Co. Rd. 14 exit off Hwy. 52. There is a
large parking lot, shelter, water and restrooms at milepost 5
from Rochester.

Trailhead north: Pine Island Park on the NE corner of Pine
Island just south of exit from Hwy. 52. Parking, restrooms,
water and picnic tables.

The Douglas Trail is one of the few in the state that can be covered in its entirety, riding both directions, in less than four hours. Its 12½ mile length combined with easy access and adequate parking at both trailheads make this an excellent half-day, one vehicle trip.

Enroute you will cross the Zumbro River and Plum Creek on wide, refurbished bridges. The trail itself is wide and in excellent condition with the only hazard being the need to cross several country gravel roads. The trail winds past a golf course and through fertile farm country. It is not heavily wooded but there is tree cover much of the way. You may encounter horseback riders as a horse and cross-country ski trail parallel the bike path and the two cross at occasional, well-marked points.

There is an interesting country store adjacent to the trail at Douglas, as well as good drinking water out of an old-fashioned hand pump located near the trail. This is also an excellent access point with parking lot.

This is a good choice for an early or late season ride when that unusually nice day comes along, but we recommend it at any time during the biking season.

Bike Shorts

• Check your tire pressure every week. Keep your tires inflated to the pressure on the side of the tire. Always check your tires before a trail ride.

• You should have a bell or a horn to alert pedestrians and other riders when passing on the left side of the trail.

ZUMBRO LAKE

Zumbro

River

Middle

Fork

12

NOCO

River

52

Zumbro

63

Fork

South

➤ Mileage
π Picnic
P Parking
W Water
S Shelter
R Restrooms
■ Rest Areas

Administered by Minnesota Department
of Natural Resources

P
S R

22

ROCHESTER

Trail length: 28 miles

Surface: Blacktop

Trailhead west: The trail begins at
Heartland Park in Park Rapids. Going east
on Hwy. 34 through Park Rapids, you turn
north on Central Avenue. There is a sign on
Central Avenue indicating the Heartland
Trail. You turn left (west) on North Street which leads right
into the park. There is a large paved lot with excellent
facilities and you may park there overnight.

In the area: Itasca State Park is just 21 miles north of Park
Rapids. There are 17 miles of bike paths in the park. Write to:

> Itasca State Park
> Lake Itasca MN 56460
> 218-266-3656
> 800-765-CAMP (2267) for accommodations.

Trailhead east: In Walker where Hwy. 34 intersects with Co.
Rd. 12. The trailhead is 3/4 mile west on Co. Rd. 12. The
parking lot with restrooms is set back from the street.

In the area: Leech Lake is located in Minnesota's heartland in
the Chippewa National Forest. For other tourist information,
write:

> Walker Leech Lake
> Walker Chamber of Commerce
> Walker MN 56484
> MN 800-247-0944

If you enjoy the north woods, glacial lakes and flowing
streams, you will like the Heartland Trail. The west trailhead
is located just 21 miles from one of the major attractions in
northern Minnesota, the Itasca State Park and the origin of
the mighty Mississippi River.

Paved in 1975, this was the first black-topped trail in Minnesota, perhaps in the country. The Heartland is a popular trail for snowmobilers in winter. The surfaced bike portion is part of many miles of trail for winter recreation which are not suitable for biking except for the real mountain bike enthusiasts. These trails do, however, offer an opportunity to get off your bicycle and just take a quiet walk in the woods.

The 28 miles of paved bike trail is an easy one-half day ride through the Chippewa State Forest and also lends itself to a two-way, one day ride. Our group prefers to ride to Walker one day and back to Park Rapids the next. This is partly because of the driving distance from home, but also because of the interesting towns, scenery, and the area in general. For overnight trips, reservations are highly recommended if you want a motel room during the tourist season.

If you plan to ride two half-days, we recommend starting at Heartland Park in Park Rapids where you may leave your car overnight. Heading east out of Park Rapids you will soon find yourself in deep woods with only an occasional farm field or residence in sight. 10.5 miles brings you into Nevis where we had lunch at a most unusual restaurant.

Another 5.5 miles puts you in Akely where you will want to ride the one block off the trail and have your picture taken while sitting on the hand of a huge Paul Bunyon statue at the municipal park on Main St. On the north side of the trail at Akely, there is a picnic shelter, tables and outdoor restrooms. A well with hand pump will give you good water.

From Akely to Walker is probably the most scenic section. You leave the proximity of Highway 34 (and its occasional residence) and ride by numerous lakes. The east end of the trail ends rather abruptly and it is necessary to ride the last 1/4 mile into Walker on city streets.

In Walker we found excellent accommodations at reasonable rates with a good family restaurant just a short distance from the marina on beautiful Leech Lake.

Administered by Minnesota Department of Natural Resources

371

Leech Lake

WALKER

R P

12

8.5 mi.

23

64

25

Eleventh Crow

Wing Lake

34

50

AKELEY

π P
W S
R

12

Big Bass

Howard
Lake

49

33

Tenmile Lake

64

➤ Mileage
π Picnic
P Parking
W Water
S Shelter
R Restrooms

Trail length: 32 miles,
                   Hinckley to Moose Lake

An additional 4.5 miles to Barnum,
        summer 1990

Surface: Blacktop

Trailhead south: Exit I-35 at Hinckley and go west to Main St. which is Hwy. 23. Turn north and continue to Co. Rd. 18, turn west across the tracks to parking lot with facilities on the Grindstone River.

In the area: The Hinckley Fire Museum, the story of an era, its people and a fire. The Mission Creek 1894 Theme Park and Tobie's restaurant are on the east side of I-35.

Trailhead north: At Moose Lake, exit I-35 at Co. Rd. 27. Drive one mile west to Hwy. 61, then south one block to parking lot.

The trailhead at Barnum is on Co. Rd. 6 on the north side of town.

Bike Shorts

• The most certain way to ride regularly is to develop a group of interested friends.

• Always carry your own water bottle. For a cool drink, fill your water bottle the night before and freeze overnight.

The Hinckley Fire Trail obviously got its name from the forest fire of 1894. This catastrophe of many years ago adds considerable interest to this ride. The trail is laid upon a rail bed which played an important role during the fire. While in Hinckley you will want to save some time to visit the Hinckley Fire Museum near downtown.

Heading north from Hinckley, you will find scattered forest or trees with considerable farm land. It is very flat with only an occasional grade except for a short, curvy stretch where they left the rail bed. This is one of the more open routes and you may want to consider wind direction when planning your trip.

Should you choose to access at a point other than the trail-heads, Finlayson, Willow River and Sturgeon Lake are all easy to get to. The bikeway stretches 32 miles between Hinckley and Moose Lake and will someday connect to the Willard Munger Trail at Carlton. Paving is planned from Moose Lake to Barnum in the summer of 1990, for an additional 4.5 miles.

If you want a 3 to 5 hour ride for your day's exercise, it will be necessary to leave a car at either end or make it an over-night stay. Good motels are available at both Moose Lake and Hinckley.

Bike Shorts

- There are 570 miles of off-road bikeways in Minnesota.

- Keep brakes, horn and other safety devices in good working condition. Brakes should be able to make the wheel skid on a dry, clean surface. Inspect your bike often for needed repairs/worn out parts.

BARNUM

6

4.5 mi.

MOOSE
LAKE

8

73 27

P

6 mi.

STURGEON
LAKE

46

4 mi.

WILLOW
RIVER

P

41

43

Willow River

Pine River

RUTLEDGE

23

5.5 mi.

P

FINLAYSON

3.5 mi.

ASKOV

GRONINGEN

SANDSTONE

4.5 mi.

North Fork Grindstone

61

FRIESLAND

35

61

Kettle River

20

➤ Mileage
P Parking
R Restrooms

4 mi.

HINCKLEY

18

R P

48

Administered by Minnesota
Department of Natural Resources

24

Trail length: 30 miles

Surface: Crushed limestone

Trailhead east: From I-494 exit west on Hwy. 12 (Wayzata Blvd.) to Co. Rd. 15 (Gleason Lake Rd.). Turn north and exit to the north on Vicksburg Lane. Continue north to 10th Ave. N. (there is a sign) and turn west 1/2 block to the parking lot with restrooms.

The City of Plymouth has paved a spur east to I-494 as part of their development of Parkers Lake.

If you are traveling west on Hwy. 55, west of I-494, turn south at Vicksburg Lane.

Mid access: Several county roads cross the trail but the only interim parking lot is at Stubbs Bay Rd. in Orono. You can access at Watertown where the trail crosses Co. Rd. 24. Street parking only.

In the area: Lake Minnetonka and the western suburbs as well as the entire Twin Cities area. More information on attractions in the area is available from:

> Twin West Chamber of Commerce
> 10550 Wayzata Blvd. #2
> Minnetonka MN 55343
> 612-540-0234

Trailhead west: The limestone surface actually ends at Co. Rd. 9 in Winsted but the parking lot is a short distance east on Lake Winsted. There is a county park with facilities at the southern tip of Lake Winsted.

This is presently the only DNR trail that originates in the metropolitan Twin Cities area and its Plymouth-Wayzata sector receives considerable use.

The Luce Line Trail actually begins at the parking lot on 10th Ave. N. just off Vicksburg Lane, but the City of Plymouth paved a short section east to I-494. The DNR trail has a firm crushed limestone and well-maintained surface that extends 30 miles west to Winsted.

Through the foresight of the Luce Line Trail Association and subsequently the State Legislature, the right of way continues west from Plymouth for 97 miles, just 55 miles short of the South Dakota border. Think of the ride it will make when complete! Mountain bikes are now able to negotiate much more of this trail than touring or racing bikes. From Winsted west there are bridges to be replaced or built and the trail evaporates for short stretches, principally in villages and towns.

Thirty miles may necessitate a two vehicle outing unless you want to make it a long trip or take only a portion of the trail. The majority of the distance is through open country with only scattered tree cover except in the Wayzata-Plymouth end. The eastern 8 or 10 miles is really the most interesting with residential sections, trees, lakes and a different view when you ride through the Wayzata Country Club.

We prefer to start at the east end but wind direction may be a consideration because it is a fairly open trail for much of the route. Although there are few towns, Lyndale is an interesting stop for refreshments. Be sure your water bottle is full and you have snacks in your pack for this trail.

LUCE LINE STATE TRAIL

Administered by Minnesota Department of Natural Resources

28

➤ Mileage
π Picnic
P Parking
R Restrooms

Trail length: 14.5 miles

Surface: Blacktop

Trailhead north: Driving north on I-35 take Grand Ave. exit in west Duluth. Follow Grand Ave. S. just past the Duluth Zoo and the Munger Motel. Turn left to parking lot.

In the area: There are many reasons to visit Duluth. Exit I-35 at the Spirit Mt. ramp and stop at the State Information Center or call:

> Duluth Visitors Bureau
> 1-800-4-DULUTH

Trailhead west: Exit from I-35 on Hwy. 210, drive east to Carlton. At the four-way stop turn onto Co. Rd. 1 and proceed about one block to the trailhead parking lot.

In the area: For information on Jay Cooke State Park, call 800-862-2370

The Willard Munger is the very northern 14.5 miles of what is eventually planned to be a single trail from St. Paul to Duluth (and perhaps beyond). When they complete the 25 to 30 miles between the end of the Willard Munger and the beginning of the Hinckley Trail what a super distance ride it will make!

The first time we selected this trail, we started at Duluth. 14.5 miles makes an easy two-way ride but the first 9 miles seem more of a grade than the 3% slope and we wanted to do that part while we were still fresh. We recommend this approach for that reason and because it permits you to start and end your ride in Duluth. While the ride up is a bit strenuous, the long coast back down makes up for it.

Along the way, there are some interesting cuts through solid rock, a great view of Lake Superior and Wisconsin, and other scenic vistas. The trail takes you through woods, alongside Jay Cooke State Park and over a high bridge overlooking a spectacular gorge where you may see park visitors swimming and fishing. We did not join them, but not much further west, we did cool off by wading into a cool, clear stream paralleling our path.

One pleasant surprise enroute was a mobile refreshment stand run by an enterprising individual complete with ice cream, pop, candy, food and picnic tables.

If you choose a one-way ride, there is ample parking one block from downtown in Carlton. Because of the long down grade, you will find the Carlton to Duluth ride will take quite a bit less time so you may want to include a side trip into Jay Cooke State Park.

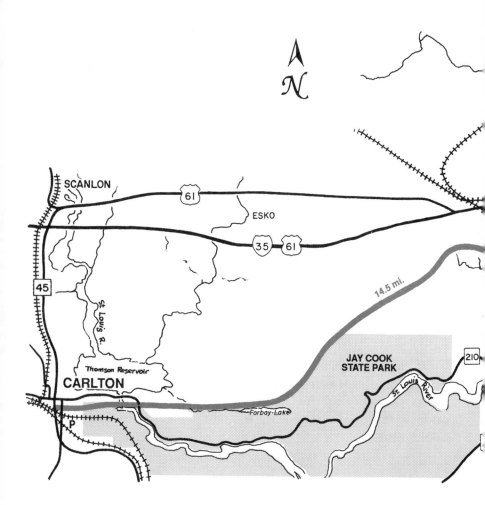

Administered by Minnesota Department of Natural Resources

DULUTH

ES
ER

2

P

23

Spirit
Lake

SUPERIOR

Fond
du Lac

23 39

P   Parking

Trail length: 31 miles

Surface: Blacktop

Trailhead west: Now located one mile east of Fountain on the south side of Co. Rd. 8. Parking and portable restrooms available. Trail extension into Fountain is in the planning stage.

Mid access: At Whalen -- permanent restrooms, picnic tables. At Lanesboro -- the trail passes through the center of town crossing Co. Rd. 250.

Access at Isinours Unit on Co. Rd. 17. The parking lot is about 1/4 mile west of Co. Rd. 17 at Isinours wood lot.

In the area: Lanesboro is a picturesque village with antique shops, a winery, campground, a historic inn and two bed and breakfast inns. An eatery on the main street has live music and wonderful food. There is a resident wood carver and Amish gift shop.

Trailhead east: Rushford's main thoroughfare is Mill St., also marked Hwy. 43. The trailhead is one block west, just past Hwy. 16 and before Hwy. 30. The depot is open year around and is being developed into a railroad and trail museum.

For information on this charming area call or write for a brochure.

> Historic Bluff Country
> P.O. Box 609, Harmony MN 55939
> 507-886-2230

Completed in 1989, The Root River Trail provides 31 paved miles along the Root River valley and through the hardwood forest and bluffs of this historic region. Consider it for an early or late season ride, but it is great any time of the year. It is one of the more level trails except at the extreme west end and a short adjustment about mid-point between Fountain and Lanesboro.

The 31 miles makes it an ideal one-way ride for the casual bicyclist, but the opportunities and attractions of this general area suggest an overnight stay at one of the several bed and breakfasts or motels along or near it. Try riding both ways on a two day excursion.

The Root River State Trail follows the watershed and general route of the south branch of its namesake between Fountain and Lanesboro and joins the main branch just east of Lanesboro. Although the trail is not always adjacent to a river, you will often see trout fisherman, canoeists and other outdoor enthusiasts on your ride. The trail includes 48 bridges with lengths of up to 500 feet. Of course, the towns of Fountain, Lanesboro and Rushford are attractions in themselves, with the entire downtown section of Lanesboro listed on the National Register of Historic Places.

The route will take you through the scenic bluffs and extensive hardwood forest of southern Minnesota. Be alert for wildlife, especially through the Lost Lake Game Refuge just west of Lanesboro. Worthwhile side trips include the State Fish Hatchery south of Lanesboro on Highway 16 or the Amish Community and shops at Harmony.

We prefer to plan this trip for a one-way ride from the west trailhead just east of Fountain to the east trailhead near downtown Rushford. The main reason is that it gives you a downhill ride all the way with one exception when the trail leaves the valley to get on top of the bluffs and return to the rail bed after a short distance.

At Fountain, there is ample parking, a shelter and portable restrooms. From this point, the trail takes an immediate downhill grade for nearly two miles until it reaches the river valley. Three miles further along you will see an old railroad building and another parking lot. This was once the point where the railroad used to put on a second engine to pull the trains up the grade you just came down. It is also the site of the Isinours Demonstration Woodland where you may want to take a walking side trip and view the many varieties of trees (labeled) with which the foresters are experimenting or are observing.

In Lanesboro, you will ride by the dam which provides electricity for the city. The trail center is located in the basement of the Lanesboro Historical Society Museum. (Clean restrooms, water, trail maps, etc.) In fact, you will ride right through the downtown section which will provide all conveniences including parking and a nearby campground should you decide to start your trip there.

Heading east, your next stop might be Whalen where they conveniently provide picnic tables and restrooms at trailside. Your next chance for refreshments is Peterson, 9 miles further east. Nearing Rushford is the only part of the trip in open country or paralleling a highway. Once in Rushford, you will find ample parking near the depot and excellent restaurants and accommodations.

If your party has chosen to drop a vehicle at both trailheads to permit a one-way ride, take Hwy. 8 from Fountain to Lanesboro and then Hwy. 16 from Lanesboro to Rushford. However you do it, this is a ride you will want to do again and again.

43

Trail
Center
RUSHFORD

30
5 mi.

R.P.

Root River

16

SOUTH RUSHFORD

π

25

105

5 mi.

16

PETERSON

16

106

43

π

25

π

4 mi.

π

➤   Mileage
π   Picnic
P   Parking
S   Shelter
R   Restrooms

WHALAN
  P R π

106

N

23

Administered by Minnesota Department of Natural Resources

37

Trail length: 39 miles

Surface: Crushed limestone

Trailhead west: North of Mankato on Hwy. 22 to Lime Valley Rd., (about) one mile north of Hwy. 22 interchange on Hwy. 14 bypass. Exit west off Hwy. 22. Parking but no facilities.

In the area: Located on the banks of the Minnesota River, Mankato is the home of Mankato State University. Minneopa Falls in Minneopa State Park is 5 miles west on Hwy. 68 and U.S. 169. You can request information from:

>
Mankato Chamber of Commerce
P.O. Box 999
Mankato MN 56002
507-345-4519

>
Minneopa State Park
Route 9, Box 143
Mankato MN 56001
507-625-4388

Mid access: At Elysian on Hwy. 60. Parking lot with new building and restrooms. At Waterville, Hwy. 13 and Hwy. 60.

Trailhead east: Exit I-35 at Hwy. 60. Trail begins on north side of Hwy. 60 just west of restaurant.

In the area: The Ivan Willock Woodcarving Studio and School is located in Faribault as are Shattuck School, the Faribault Alexander House and the Rice County Historical Society. More information is available from:

>
Faribault Chamber of Commerce
P.O. Box 434
Faribault MN 55021
507-334-4381

A crushed limestone trail, Sakatah Singing Hills traverses part of three counties along its 39 miles. This level trail wanders near lush pastures and farmland, along several lakes, through three small towns and a forested state park. There are swimming beaches within a short ride off the trail at Sakatah Lake State Park, Waterville, Elysian, Madison Lake, and Cannon Lake. The fish hatchery in Waterville is open to visitors.

As yet, the trail has relatively few improvements such as picnic tables and rest stops, but with the several small towns and Sakatah State Park, restrooms and water are not hard to come by.

Thirty nine miles makes a pretty good one day ride so you may want to leave a car at Faribault if the wind is westerly, or at Mankato if the wind is easterly.

If you are campers as well as bikers, Sakatah State Park is 14 miles from the Faribault trailhead. In our group opinion, the east 14 miles is the most scenic as well as the most shaded and would make an excellent two way ride.

One should consider the lakeside town of Elysian as a starting point for both portions of the trail. It is very near the half-way point and has an excellent parking lot and shelter with restrooms and water.

FARIBAULT

35

11

38

Cedar L.

12

Well L.

13

Carmon Lake

13

P

WARSAW

18

14 mi.

Sakatah Lake

onka Lake

15

VATERVILLE

MORRISTOWN

SAKATAH LAKE
STATE PARK

16

0

.5 mile severance

13

➤ Mileage
P Parking
■ Rest Areas

N

WASECA

Administered by Minnesota
Department of Natural Resources

PART III

STATE PARKS

REGIONAL PARKS

HENNEPIN PARKS

MINNEAPOLIS
PARKS and RECREATION

ST. PAUL
PARKS and RECREATION

Many state and regional parks provide excellent bike paths as a part of their facilities. Although often short, they are well worth considering as a part of your family outing or for a short ride any time.

Minnesota has 65 state parks. Eleven provide designated bike paths as listed below.

Afton — From St. Paul, go 8 miles east on I-94, then 7 miles south on Co. Rd. 15, 3 miles east on Co. Rd. 20
4 mile bike path

Camden — On State Highway 23, ten miles south of Marshall
4 mile bike path

Ft. Snelling — Take Post Rd. off State Hwy. 5
5 mile bike path

Itasca — 21 miles north of Park Rapids on U.S. Hwy. 71
17 mile bike path (detailed description on page 46)

Lake Bemidji — 1.7 miles off old U.S. 71 on State Hwy. 20
1 mile bike path

Minneopa — 5 miles west of Mankato on State Hwy. 68 and U.S. 169
4 mile bike path

Minnesota Valley — Off U.S. Hwy. 169 west of Jordon
4 mile bike path

St. Croix — 16 miles east of Hinckley on State Hwy. 48
6.5 mile bike path

Sakatah — 14 miles west of Faribault on Hwy. 60
The Sakatah Singing Hills State Trail passes through the park (see page 38).

Sibley — 15 miles north of Willmar on U.S. Hwy. 71
5 mile bike path

William O'Brien — State Hwy. 95, two miles north of Marine-
-on-St. Croix
2 mile bike path

This information is from *Minnesota State Parks - Naturally* available from the Department of Natural Resources Information Center, 500 Lafayette Road, St. Paul MN 55155. The Center is open Monday through Friday 8:00 a.m. to 4:30 p.m. You can visit the Information Center or order by mail. Telephone in Minnesota toll free 800-652-9747, ask for DNR.

ITASCA STATE PARK

Trail length: 17 miles

Surface: Paved

Here is a chance to combine a really scenic
bike ride with a visit to one of the more famous
state parks in the nation. Not only is the scenery impressive,
but the park offers a wide variety of other attractions. In
April, 1991, this park will celebrate its 100th birthday.

The off-road bike path is only 6.5 miles, with an additional 10.5
designated on low traffic roads. **Bike rentals are available
in the park.** The south trailhead starts at the information
center on the east entrance road, and the north trailhead starts
in the parking lot for the interpretive center at the headwaters
of the Mississippi River near the north entrance road.

The location lends itself well to a companion trip with the
Heartland Trail (see page 18). Biking enthusiasts may want to
consider staying in Park Rapids or riding to Park Rapids. It is
only 20 miles via U.S. Highway 71 from the south edge of the
park. The highway has paved shoulders specifically marked
for biking or hiking and it would be an interesting ride.

The virgin pines, lakes and other attractions of the park make
this trail a real gem for the outdoor enthusiast and nature lover.
Be sure of your reservations, including campgrounds, during the
summer season. For reservations as well as general information
about the park contact:

> Itasca State Park Manager
> Lake Itasca MN 56460
> 218-266-3654
> 800-765-2267

Mississippi R.

P

P

P

Mississippi River
Headwaters
Interpretive Tours
Programs – Trails
Gifts

P

P

200

Lake Itasca

Itasca
Wilderness
Sanctuary

Bicycle
Rental

East Arm

N

P Parking

38

46

Lyndecker

Douglas
Lodge

P

Forest Inn
Visitor Center

1

Elk
Lake

P

Mary L.

The Metropolitan Council publishes a comprehensive map and guide to regional parks in the following seven counties: Carver, Dakota, Hennepin, Ramsey, Washington, Anoka and Wright.

Of the parks detailed in the guide, the following have designated biking paths:

Anoka County Riverfront ⌐
Long Lake   Detailed maps
Lake Elmo   unavailable. See
Battle Creek   publication below.
Rice Creek West ⌐

This publication *A Map and Guide to Regional Parks in the Twin Cities Area* is available free of charge.

Metropolitan Council
230 East Fifth Street
St. Paul MN 55101
612-291-6359

Bunker Hills Regional Park
Hennepin County Park Reserve District (Anoka)
Trail Length — 5.5 miles, paved

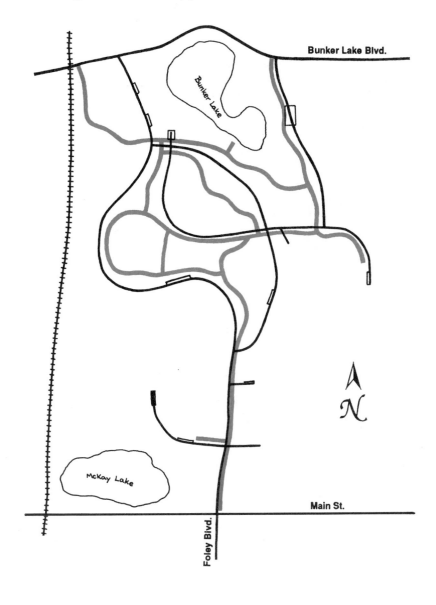

Baker Park Reserve
Trail Length — 6.2 miles, paved

Located approximately 20 miles west of downtown Minneapolis
on County Road 19, between Highway 12 and Highway 55. From
Highway 12, take County Road 29 north to County Road 19, and
follow 19 north to the main park entrance. From Highway 55,
take County Road 24 west to County Road 19, turn south and
follow 19 to the main park entrance, or take Highway 55 to
County Road 19, turn south and follow 19 to the main entrance.
Phone: 479-2258 (Gate) or 476-4666 (Office)

Carver Park Reserve

Trail Length — 7.65 miles, paved

Located in Victoria, on Carver County Road 11. Take Highway 7 west from Minneapolis and turn left on County Road 11. Or take Highway 5 west from Minneapolis and turn right on County Road 11.
Phone: 446-9474 (Gate)

Cleary Lake Regional Park
Trail Length — 3.5 miles, paved

Located near Prior Lake on Scott County Road 27. From Interstate 35W, go west on County Road 42, then south on County Road 27. Or take Interstate 494 to County Road 18, go south on 18 to Highway 101, then east to Highway 13, south on 13 to County Road 42, east on 42 to County Road 27, and south on 27 to the park entrance.
Phone: 447-2171 (Recreation Center)

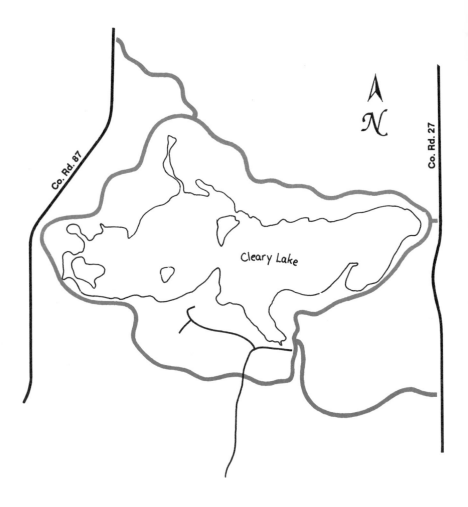

Elm Creek Park Reserve

Trail Length — 9.3 miles, paved (Also a 6.5 mile paved North
Hennepin Trail corridor connects the Elm Creek trails with
the Coon Rapids Dam.)

Located northwest of Osseo, between the communities of Champlin,
Dayton and Maple Grove. For the recreation area, take County Road 81 to
Territorial Road. Turn right and follow to the park entrance.
Phone: 424-5511 (Recreation Center)

Hyland Lake Park Reserve
Trail Length — 5.5 miles, paved

Located on East Bush Lake Road in
Bloomington. From Interstate 494, go
south on Normandale Blvd. (Highway
100) to 84th St. Turn right and follow
84th St. to East Bush Lake Road.
Go south on East Bush Lake Road
and follow the signs to Richardson
Nature Center and Hyland
Outdoor Recreation Center.
Phone: 941-4362 (Rec. Center)

54

Lake Rebecca Park Reserve
Trail Length — 6.5 miles, paved

Located approximately 30 miles west of Minneapolis on
County Road 50. Take Highway 55 west to County Road 50,
turn left and follow to the park entrance.
Phone: 972-2620 (Trailhead)

North Hennepin Trail Corridor

Trail Length — 7.2 miles (also connects to the 9.3 mile Elm Creek trail), paved

Very flat trail connecting Elm Creek Park Reserve and Coon Rapids Dam Regional Park. Access from either park or several locations along the trail.

Grand Rounds Parkway System
Trail Length — 37.9 miles, paved

The system includes: the Chain of Lakes, Lake Nokomis, and Lake Hiawatha; Minnehaha, Shingle, and Bassett Creeks; and the Mississippi River.

Shingle Creek

Wirth Memorial Parkway

Mississippi River

Olson Hwy.

Theodore Wirth

Cedar

Franklin

Central Mississippi Waterfront

Hennepin Ave.

Lake St.

Lake Calhoun

Mississippi Gorge

Minnehaha Ave.

Mississippi River

Hiawatha Ave.

Mpls. Chain of Lakes

Lake Harriet

Minnehaha Pkwy.

Lake Nokomis

Nokomis - Hiawatha

Crosstown

57

Como Park
Trail Length — 1.8 miles, paved

Crosby Farm/Hidden Falls
Trail Length — 5 miles, paved

Phalen
Trail Length — 2.9 miles, paved

PART IV

WESTERN
WISCONSIN

Trail length: 32 miles

Surface: Crushed limestone

Trailhead west: Exit I-90 at Hwy. 27, Sparta.
Follow Johns St. to 9th Lane (in S.E. corner of
Sparta). Continue south to parking and
camping on left of road. Follow the signs.

Mid access: Norwalk on Hwy. 71 & Co. Rd. T (trail mile 11.9)
Wilton on Hwy. 71 & Co. Rd. M (trail mile 17.3)
Kendall on Hwy. 71 & Co. Rd. W (trail mile 26.4)
Trail headquarters is located at Kendall, 5.7 miles from east
trailhead.

In the area: Kendall's annual Labor Day weekend celebration
features a parade, dance, and plenty of barbecued chicken and
sweet corn.
In Wilton the Lions Club serves pancake breakfasts in
the municipal park Sunday mornings from June to September.
Sparta has a 34 acre lake.

Trailhead east: The west edge of Elroy just north of Hwy. 71.
There is a public campground just south of Hwy. 71 and the
trailhead.

The foresight of responsible individuals and the State of Wisconsin has provided us with a truly exceptional bike trail in an unusually scenic area. It has been maintained and in use since 1965 and has become well known nationally among biking enthusiasts.

The Elroy-Sparta Trail traverses the Hidden Valley country of Wisconsin providing spectacular scenery as well as great bird watching and possible wildlife sightings. (The entire trail is a wildlife refuge.) The area is heavily wooded, providing shelter from sun and wind. The woods also make this an extremely popular ride during the fall color season in the state.

The rugged and scenic attraction of the area probably tells you this trail is not the level or gradually inclined roadbed of the prairie or river bottom. In fact, there are few level stretches, with long, rather steep (for a railbed) inclines. The long upgrades are matched by equally long downgrades that give you the chance to rest up. This trail does, however, require more physical conditioning and stamina than most 32 mile rides.

There are three upgrades, each leading to a tunnel cut through solid rock. Those tunnels make the trail unique. Tunnel 3 (at mile 12.4 from west end) is .7 miles long. Tunnel 2 (at 19.5 miles) is .3 miles long and tunnel 1 (at mile 25.3) is .25 miles long. For tunnel 3, special equipment not taken along on most bike trips is highly recommended. A 3/4 mile tunnel is long and dark and you will need a flashlight. You may need an extra wrap as tunnels can be both cold and damp. You will need to walk your bike at least through tunnel 3, so it will take awhile. The spirit of adventure provided by the tunnels really adds something special to this trip.

In the valleys between each tunnel (as well as at each end) are interesting small towns that truly welcome bikers and provide food, refreshments and restrooms. Of special interest is the refurbished depot at Kendall which has been designated a national historic landmark. It also serves as the trail headquarters and as a railroad museum.

For the casual or weekend biker, a one-way trip is a full day ride. This necessitates staying overnight or dropping a car at one end. Should your party want to drop a car, Hwy. 71 parallels the trail all the way. If you have only one vehicle, this is one of the few trails that provides a driver service. Take two sets of keys with you and pick up a driver at the Kendall headquarters. The driver will drop you at your start point and return your car to Kendall. There is a nominal fee and reservations are recommended.

For further information contact:

Kendall Depot
Bike Trail Headquarters
P.O. Box 153
Kendall WI 54638
Phone 608-463-7109

Trail length: 14.5 miles

Surface: Crushed limestone

Trailhead north: On Hwy. 29 in west
Menominee at Riverside Park on the west side
of the Red Cedar River.

Mid access: Irvington on Hwy. D (mile 2.7)
Downsville on Hwy. 25 (mile 7.5)
Dunnville on Hwy. Y (mile 12.5)

Trailhead south: Trail ends after crossing Chippewa River on
800 ft. trestle. Access would be Dunnville.

In the area: The Downsville Cooperative Creamery was
founded in 1904 and currently houses a restaurant, lounge,
four room inn, as well as showroom and shop for the Dunn
County Pottery.

In Menominee, the Tinman Triathalon takes place Labor Day
Weekend.

For more information about the area, contact:

Greater Menomonie Area
Chamber of Commerce
335 Main Street
P.O. Box 246
Menomonie WI 54751
715-235-9087

We want to include the Red Cedar as one of our Vikingland trails, not only because it is the Wisconsin trail closest to the Twin Cities, but also because of its uniqueness and the many attractions of the area.

As with all Wisconsin trails, it is well-maintained crushed limestone. You will pass through woodlands and prairies and past unique rock formations. For most of its distance, the trail overlooks the Red Cedar River, also popular with canoeists. Several picnic tables have been provided in scenic spots where you can rest and relax.

Although the southern trailhead ends rather abruptly just after you cross the Chippewa River, don't miss going over. We found the wide and sandy shores of the Chippewa to be an excellent picnic spot, plus you get the opportunity to ride perhaps the longest trestle (800 ft.) on any bike trail and enjoy a spectacular view in the process.

Since its total length is only 14.5 miles, it is a very manageable two-way ride no matter where you start. Give yourself some extra time for this one because there are so many interesting things to see and do along the way.

Bike Shorts

- Adults today are very health conscious and bicycling is one of the best forms of exercise.

- When you have children with you, take extra water.

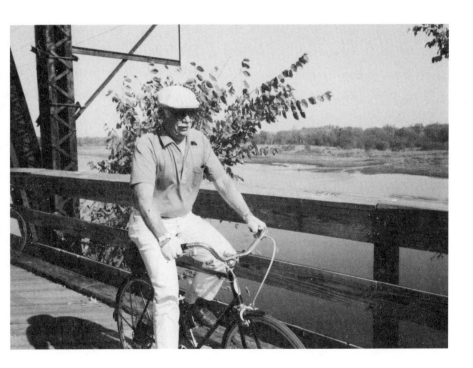

PART V

SAFETY
AND
EQUIPMENT

Fortunately, accidents and injury are not common in cycling, especially beyond the exuberance of youth. But they do happen and certainly detract from the enjoyment of a bike trip.

Common sense and awareness are the best policy. Even the most experienced among us can benefit from a periodic refresher course on the subject, so following are some safety tips that should be stored in everyone's memory bank:

Common Sense:
1.   Obey traffic laws and obey traffic signs. Most serious accidents involve motor vehicles and drivers are conditioned to expect you to do as another motor vehicle would.

2.   Go with the traffic flow, signal your turns and lane changes and be especially alert for pedestrians or car doors opening when passing a line of parked cars or other roadside obstructions. Stay as close to the right side of the road as possible.

3.   Yield the right-of-way to vehicles or pedestrians. Be prepared to do so even if you have the right-of-way. A bicycle is hardly the vehicle for practicing that a good offense is the best defense.

4.   Wear an approved helmet. This is one of the most important precautions you can take to avoid serious injury. (See Mayo Clinic article on the subject, page 74.)

5.   Plan your ride so you are off the streets, roads and trails by dusk. Bicycles are best left parked or stored at night, but if you must, be sure you have front, side and rear reflectors, plus lights. Wear or switch to light-colored clothing.

6.   Give an audible signal (we recommend a bike bell) before passing pedestrians or other cyclists.

Awareness:

1. Give your bike a pre-ride check. This is not only for maintenance. Good brakes and a mechanically sound bike are necessary for maximum safety and enjoyment. Check your tire pressure every week. Keep your tires inflated to the pressure noted on the side of the tire.

2. When planning a trip, be aware of your own capabilities as well as the limitations and health of your friends. A ride which tests one's outer limits is best left to those conditioned to do so.

3. Be alert to changing conditions. Rain will muffle the sound of approaching vehicles and generate slippery conditions, especially after a long period without rain. (Roadway oil and grime can be hazardous until the rain washes them away.)

4. Watch for road debris or loose rocks or gravel. Slow down if there is excessive debris or broken road surface. Learn to guide your bike very straight and vertical through loose sand or rocks. If you find a short stretch of loose sand it would even pay to practice riding through it a few times to give you needed confidence when it surprises you along the trail.

5. The old Irish prayer "May the wind blow always at your back" is only partially true for bicyclists. Be prepared for the vacuum effect of passing vehicles, sudden gusts or sudden absences when passing roadside buildings, trees or other shelter.

6. A word about dogs, many of whom seem to take particular objection to bicycles. If you encounter one, the first requirement is not to panic. If the dog is only testing, and not actually attacking, a shout or order may keep it at bay. If it is very aggressive, the best defense is to dismount, keeping the bike between you and the dog. Grab anything available to throw or pretend to throw. Most of all, keep moving as a dog is only going to defend what it perceives to be the limits of its territory.

Bicycle helmets*

Protective headgear can be a lifesaver
It's as easy as falling off a bicycle.

The adage has been around for decades. Unfortunately, it makes light of the potential for tragedy if you should take a serious fall while riding a bicycle.

With an increasing number of people riding bicycles on our streets and highways, the risk of injury — in particular, head injury — continues to rise. Each year, nearly 50,000 bicyclists suffer serious head injuries. According to the most recent statistics, head injuries are the leading cause of death in the approximately 1,300 bicycle-related fatalities that occur annually. To a large extent, these head injuries are preventable.

Wearing a helmet can make a difference
Until recently, advocates of the use of protective headgear for cyclists found their stance lacked scientific support. But wearing protective headgear clearly makes a difference. Recent evidence confirms that a helmet can reduce your risk of serious head and brain injury by almost 90 percent should you be involved in a bicycle accident.

Factors that can lead to head injury
Don't let common myths lull you into a false sense of security regarding your risk of head injury while riding a bicycle.

Myth: "Head injuries only happen to kids."
Fact: Only half of all brain and head injuries occur in teenagers and young children.

Myth: "I only ride in safe areas."
Fact: While most serious accidents involving bicycle riders occur on paved roads or bicycle paths, they even can occur on grass.

Myth: "I never ride fast enough to be injured."
Fact: Nearly half of all the accidents resulting in head and
    brain injuries caused no damage to the bicycle.

Bicycle riding is an excellent form of aerobic exercise that
can benefit your musculoskeletal and cardiovascular systems.
Make the investment in a helmet and take the time to put it on
each time you ride.

What to look for in a bicycle helmet
We endorse these guidelines for bicycle helmets recommended by the American Academy of Pediatrics:

● The helmet should meet the voluntary testing standards
of one of these two groups: American National Standards
Institute (ANSI) or Snell Memorial Foundation. Look for a
sticker on the inside of the helmet.

● Select the right size. Find one that fits comfortably and
doesn't pinch.

● Buy a helmet with a durable outer shell and a
polystyrene liner. Be sure it allows adequate ventilation.

● Use the adjustable foam pads to ensure a proper fit at
the front, back and sides.

● Adjust the strap for a snug fit. The helmet should cover
the top of your forehead and not rock side to side or back and
forth with the chin strap in place.

● Replace your helmet if it is involved in an accident.

---

* Reprinted from July 1989 "Mayo Clinic Health Letter" with permission of Mayo
Foundation, for Medical Education and Research, Rochester, Minnesota 55060

The proper equipment for our intended level of biking is an important factor in your safety and enjoyment. All bike shops offer a wide selection of equipment, accessories and clothing and can best advise you on your specific needs.

Basic Equipment

1. The bicycle should fit your body size. The seat and handle-bars should be adjusted to give you the maximum comfort for an extended trip. Your bike shop professional will help you with this.

2. Touring seats and handlebars are more comfortable for casual biking. Racing handlebars put considerable pressure on wrists and hands in addition to the strain on your neck from riding with your hands so low. Touring seats are wider and generally carry more padding -- something most people appreciate. You can buy seat pads filled with gel or made of soft and comfortable sheepskin.

3. The angle of the seat is critical. It should be level and the height set so the leg is nearly fully extended when the pedal is in the full down position.

Accessories

Realizing there are a multitude of accessories available, we will confine our comments to a very few which we have found to be most beneficial to our biking safety and pleasure. The most important, the helmet, is discussed at length on page 74.

1. Seat pads filled with gel provide multiple return on the investment in the form of added comfort.

2. Padded bike shorts reduce chafing, absorb moisture and provide additional padding.

3. Helmet rear view mirror is primarily a safety accessory but it also saves neck strain.

4. Padded gloves help reduce discomfort of weight and tension on the hands when subject to long periods in the same position.

5. Frame mounted water bottle should be translucent to keep track of supply.

Special Equipment

It is not necessary for certain equipment to be carried by everyone, but it is desirable for someone in the group carry a tire pump, patching material and some basic tools.

For example:
> Screwdriver
> 6" or 8" adjustable wrench
> Pair of small pliers
> Accurate tire pressure gauge

Everyone should carry at least one bike bag. How many, size and style depend on the type of ride and length of trip you intend to make.

We recommend a handle bar bag for clothing and personal items on every bike. One insulated rear wheel bag is adequate for every two people. This may require a rear carrier bracket. Use one or two reusable containers of frozen liquid to ensure cold drinks and preserve food.

If your bike trip is an overnight, you will require larger saddle bag storage for extra clothing. Saddle bags are for available either front or back wheels.

Transportation

There are a multitude of ways to transport your bicycle. Those who own a van, enclosed truck or motorhome, have a convenient as well as secure method. Roof top and rear trunk or bumper racks are perhaps the most common with only the more expensive providing theft security.

When a group is traveling some distance to a biking destination, the number of vehicles becomes a factor. It may be desirable for each vehicle to transport 4 or more bikes, or to have a unit which will transport a number of bikes.

Our group accomplishes this by having a mid-size open pickup and an open trailer available. Each will hold 4 bikes using built-in racks and rubber tie downs. The trailer also works well with any auto with a trailer hitch. This does not provide the best security so it may be necessary to take your bike indoors with you if staying overnight.

Bike Shorts

• A large plastic garbage bag takes little space and makes good emergency rain cover.

• A perfect ride begins with the right safety gear and supplies.
